Sand Tiger Shark

Sand Tiger Shark

By Carol Carrick • Illustrated by Donald Carrick

A Clarion Book • The Seabury Press • New York

*We are grateful to Thomas H. Lineaweaver III,
Marine Biological Laboratory, Woods Hole,
Massachusetts, for his technical and editorial
help.*

The Seabury Press, 815 Second Avenue, New York,
New York 10017

Library of Congress Cataloging in Publication Data

Carrick, Carol.   Sand tiger shark.
"A Clarion book."
Summary: Examines the life cycle of a sand tiger
shark.
1. Sand tiger sharks—Juvenile literature.
[1. Sand tiger sharks. 2. Sharks] I. Carrick, Donald.
II. Title.
QL638.95.03C37   597'.31   76-40206
ISBN 0-8164-3183-3

For Christopher

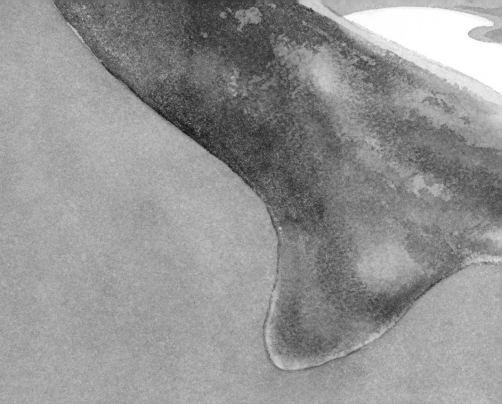

There was a natural law in the shallow nursery ground where the sand tiger shark was born. Only mothers about to give birth would enter, and while they were there none of them would eat. In this way, the newborn pup was protected from the adult sharks and not eaten, even by his own mother.

But the eating had started in the sand tiger's life before he was born . . . soon after he and a twin had hatched inside their mother. They swam inside of her for the next year, eating the other eggs that her body produced.

At birth the shark was a miniature of his mother. Already thirty inches long, and armed with dangerous teeth, he was well-equipped to leave her and his twin to fend for himself.

Swimming used little of the sand tiger's energy, but he had to keep on the move. Lacking the air sac that keeps fish afloat, he had to swim or he would sink. He also had to keep moving in order to breathe. As he swam, water was forced through his mouth, over gills that removed the oxygen he needed, and out gill slits behind his head.

After a good meal it wasn't necessary for the sand tiger to eat for a long time. Food could remain undigested in his body for weeks. But his behavior was unpredictable. His curiosity could be triggered by the sounds of fish swimming or by light reflected from their scales, and this curiosity often led to an attack.

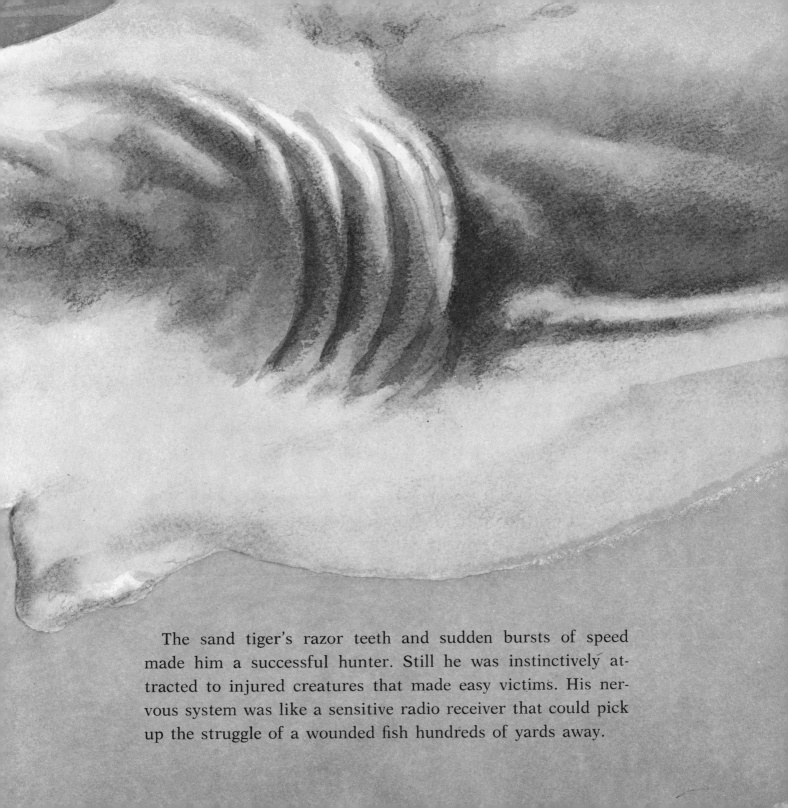

The sand tiger's razor teeth and sudden bursts of speed made him a successful hunter. Still he was instinctively attracted to injured creatures that made easy victims. His nervous system was like a sensitive radio receiver that could pick up the struggle of a wounded fish hundreds of yards away.

When the faintest smell of blood from as far as a quarter
of a mile reached the shark's acute nose, he became keenly
alert. Sweeping his head from side to side he could locate his
prey by scent alone. Then his gills flared as he sped like a
torpedo to his target.

As soon as he saw the fish's bright shimmer he circled it
cautiously, one eye always on his prey. His circles became
faster and tighter until he bumped the fish with his snout. His
rough skin, covered with tiny tooth-like scales, contained
nerve cells connected to nerve cells in his mouth. They told
him whether this wriggling object was what he wanted.

He would lunge at the fish with a terrible snap of his jaws.
Sometimes he missed. The fish might thrust one of its fins
straight out and make a quick turn. Since the shark's fins
were not flexible, but were mainly used for steering up and
down, he could not stop short or make a sudden turn. He
would have to circle for another pass at the fish.

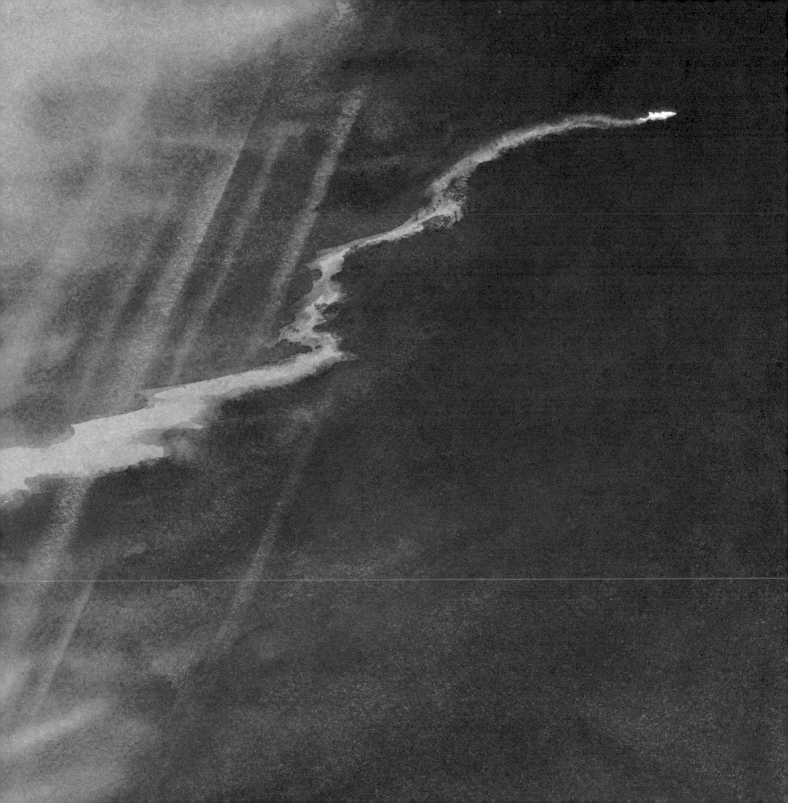

Every Spring, after the sand tiger had reached the length of seven feet, he stopped feeding and was drawn toward shore to select a mate. Often the female he favored did not seem willing. His fashion of winning her was to slash at her fins and sides, but the wounds were not meant to be serious.

Finally, the female would accept the sand tiger so he could release his sperm into a canal in her body. During this time she swam so closely with the sand tiger that they appeared to be one shark with two heads. Although her body produced many eggs, the sperm would cause only two eggs at a time to ripen.

Just as he never again saw his mother after his own birth, the sand tiger never again saw any of his mates. But a year later each of them would give birth to his pups.

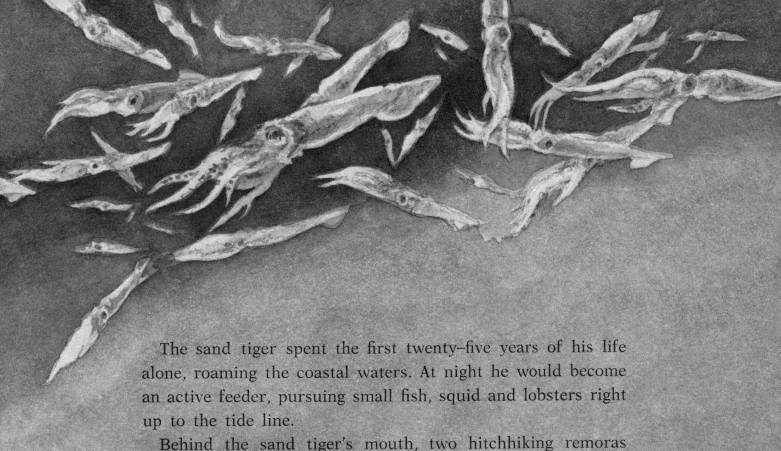

The sand tiger spent the first twenty-five years of his life alone, roaming the coastal waters. At night he would become an active feeder, pursuing small fish, squid and lobsters right up to the tide line.

Behind the sand tiger's mouth, two hitchhiking remoras hung by suction discs on top of their heads. He never bothered them or a flotilla of pilot fish that snatched at leftovers from his meals.

Then, as the shark grew older, he hung about the edge of a large school of sand tigers. He could always be recognized by his battered fins and the many scars he had received from the teeth and sharp tails and fins of other sharks. When young, all the sharks had tended to be bold, but this sand tiger, who was now ten feet long, continued to be aggressive. If another shark invaded what he felt to be his territory, the old one warned with his swimming pattern and his posture that he would defend himself.

The school of sand tigers patrolled deeper water, preying on fish imprisoned in nets. Or they attacked schools of fish and drove them into the shallows. The thrashing of fish they crippled provoked the sharks to make further raids. And when one shark moved in fast, the old sand tiger still tried to rush ahead for the first bite.

One morning the sand tigers were harassing a school of bluefish. Like a pack of wolves, the sharks made frequent rushes at the fish, attacking the slow and the weak that lagged behind.

The sand tigers felt the vibrations from a fishing boat. Then the sound of the engines stopped as the boat was allowed to drift.

The fishermen had sighted the school of bluefish. They dumped overboard a mixture of ground up fish called chum that was carried away in a continuous line by the tidal currents. The particles of blood and pulp that the fishermen poured into the sea were meant to lure the fish to their baited hooks.

As the fleeing fish streamed past the fishing boat, one of the blues seized a baited hook and raced away with it. Following in its wake, keeping a careful distance from the battling fish, was the the nose of the old sand tiger.

Not until the exhausted bluefish was being hauled into the boat did the sand tiger strike, swallowing bait, fish and hook. The surprised fisherman and the startled shark both caught more than they had expected. But with a sweep of his tail the five hundred pound sand tiger snapped the line and was free.

Picking up the scent, more sharks appeared. The sea began to cloud with blood and foam as it was crisscrossed with hurtling shadows. The fishermen abandoned their sport to watch in horror as the water boiled and discolored with the bodies of half-eaten fish who broke the surface trying to escape their pursuers.

As the oily bait, chum and bluefish mingled, the sharks grew confused about the source of the strong food smell. They now became the victims of their own savagery.

The old sand tiger bore down on a bluefish at the same time as three other sharks. Even though they were surrounded by hundreds of panicked bluefish, the crazed sharks began to slash at each other. One of the sand tiger's fins was almost torn away and blood was trailing from a gash in his side. So great was his excitement that he probably never felt his wounds. With his usual daring, the sand tiger broke away with the fish all the sharks tried to possess, and the others followed him in close pursuit.

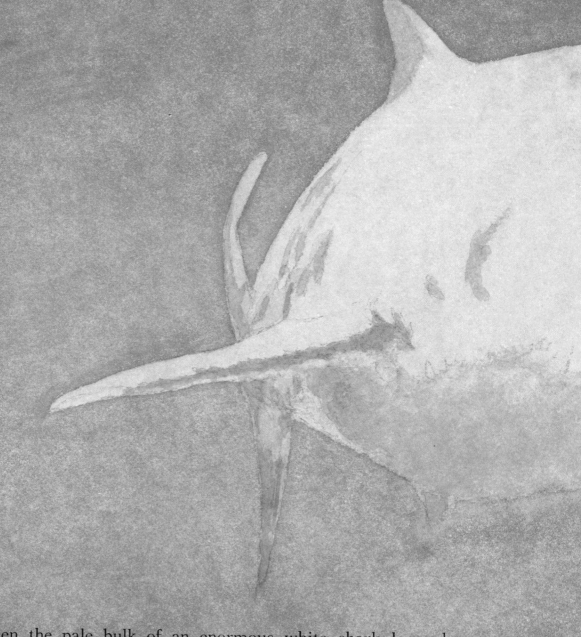

Then the pale bulk of an enormous white shark loomed through the murky water. The frenzied smaller sharks did not make way for the lord of the sea until the great white had ripped a chunk from the side of the old sand tiger.

Each time the white shark returned to make another strike his snout drew up and his jaws gaped so wide they seemed to dislocate. His sharp, triangular teeth punctured the sand tiger's tough hide, and with a jerk he tore out fifteen-pound chunks of meat. He swallowed them whole, convulsively shaking his head and body. Some of the white shark's teeth broke off, but soon they would be replaced from the extra rows lying along his inner jaw.

The remoras had released their grip on the sand tiger. They shared the last floating scraps with the scattered pilot fish.

As suddenly as the feeding frenzy began, it ended. The sea calmed and cleared. The white shark and his new escort of gaily striped pilot fish gracefully circled with round, well-filled bellies. The surviving bluefish and sand tigers regrouped, fading in different directions.

Nothing remained of the old sand tiger. But day and night his kind would continue to prowl the ocean without sleep, just as their ancestors had long before the dinosaurs, and before flowers and trees.

To breathe and to stay afloat the sharks were compelled
to wander forever. But swimming was effortless and hunting
would always be good.